PUT YOUR BIG GIRL PANTIES ON

Alexandria Cobb

Woman Up!
©2021 Alexandria Cobb
Published by: Alexandria Cobb

ISBN: 978-0-578-93565-2
Library of Congress number: 2021912152

All rights reserved, printed in the United States of America. No part of this book may be used or reproduced in any manner whatsoever without written permission, except in the case of brief quotations embodied in reports, articles, and reviews.

Edited by: Keyoka Kinzy
Cover and Interior Layout: Write on Promotions

Dedication

I would like to dedicate this book to my amazing husband, Pastor John D. Cobb II. Your love has healed me in places that I didn't even realize was broken. You have been my biggest motivator and the best coach who always "puts me in the game". I couldn't imagine life without you. Thank you for praying for me, pushing me, and propelling me to live out my God given purpose. I acknowledge and accept that I was born on purpose, for a purpose because of you.

I appreciate you allowing me the space and freedom to "BE". When I wanted to give up, you wouldn't let me. When I wanted to quit, you wouldn't let me. When I wanted to procrastinate, you wouldn't let me. You are more than what I wanted and exactly what I needed. Thank you for making this thing called life so amazing. I love you with all of me.

Introduction

Have you ever found yourself saying "this can't be life"? Life can deal you cards that you never would have thought. However, you don't have to allow what happens to you to deter you from continuing forward. You should learn and grow from every experience that happens in your life. You "grow" through life as you "go" through life.

I wrote this book to encourage every woman who feels like they are lost and have no hope. Hey girl, I've been in that place before. It's hard, lonely, and depressing. Yet, there is still life left to be lived. It starts with you making an intentional decision to choose better. God didn't intend for you to live like that, but he created to you live an abundant life that is full of love, joy, peace, and happiness. Guess what? It all starts with you. You have the power to set the tone and direction of your life. When you know better, you do better. This book was written to assist you in determining the "why" factors in your life such as:

Why am I here?

Why am I going through this?

Why me?

Why can't I get it together?

You know all the questions that we as women ask ourselves. The only way to fix the problem is to get to the root of the issue.

Most of the time, we think the issue is everyone else, but it is really ourselves. You must be the change you want to see. If you be honest, change can be very challenging and requires the fortitude to press forward and keep going. The good news is that YOU GOT WHAT IT TAKES! If you are still breathing, change is possible, and you must embrace it. It may not always feel good, but it will work for your good.

Remember, tough times build tough people.

Hey girl, it's time to Woman and put your big girl panties on. The life you want and deserve is waiting for you. Up

Chapter 1

The Ties That Break

What is a soul tie? It's a linkage that ties two souls together in the spirit realm. Soul ties can be healthy within a marriage and unhealthy outside of a marriage. Soul ties can do things, such as allow one person to manipulate and control another person without their knowledge. When that person is unaware, it allows a cycle of dysfunction to continue.

When you have sex with someone outside the context of marriage, an ungodly soul tie is formed. The soul tie can fragment the soul and become destructive. People who have had many past relationships may find it difficult to bond or connect with others because their soul is fragmented. It makes them vulnerable to poor connections.

Soul ties can create a constant tug of war between your mind and your heart. The rational part (your mind) has told you to leave and has found the nearest exit. The emotional side of you, which is flawed due to an unhealthy soul tie, makes you want to stay. Soul ties create a bond that can't be easily broken.

When your soul is tied to someone in a harmful way, it will drain everything around you. It will literally suck the life out of you and from you. The best way to tell if you are connected to a person in a destructive and negative way is to monitor how you feel around them. Are your emotions altered? Does your mood change? If so, you have a soul tie that is detrimental to your life.

When you tie yourself to the wrong person, it is one of the most influential love lessons you will learn. It will cause you to settle for less than what you deserve and tolerate more than you should. You also become blind and distracted by things that don't mean you any good. Have you ever been with someone and wanted to leave but something wouldn't let you? If so, girl, that's a soul tie!

There was a point in my life where I had soul ties to several men at the same time. I would have sex with one guy and move onto the next without being healed from the previous guy. I felt numb to my own feelings and had an altered perception of love. I was so confused about who I was, who I was with, and what I was even doing. After each sexual encounter, it left me broken. I gave a piece of myself every time I laid down with a man, only to get up still feeling unfulfilled and empty.

Now, I know you are wondering if it'll ever be possible to overcome soul ties, and the answer is absolutely. It will not happen overnight, but you can definitely do it. You have to be willing and intentional. There may be places you cannot go, people you cannot see, or things you cannot do because it will only lead you right back to the soul tie you are trying to break. You will not be able to do it on your own. You will need to ask God to give you the strength, discipline, and consistency to endure the process. Hey girl, it will not be easy, but it will be worth it.

Chapter 7 Affirmations

The Ties That Break

- I cut all ungodly soul ties between myself and any person, place, or thing that is not conducive to my life.

- I cut all ungodly soul ties created by sexual relationships, known or unknown, remembered or forgotten soul ties in Jesus name.

- I release myself from all negative soul ties, spiritual and mental agreements, and covenants with past relationships.

- I release forgiveness to sexual partners who have emotionally, spiritually or physically abused me.

- I decree a complete breakage and severing from all relationships that are unproductive, unfruitful, and ungodly in the name of Jesus.

- I declare ungodly covenants made through sexual unions to be abolished in my life, in the name of Jesus.

- I speak and decree my complete deliverance and freedom from ungodly soul ties in Jesus name.

Chapter 2

Love vs. Lust

What is love? Love is a complex set of emotions, behaviors, and beliefs that are associated with strong feelings of affection, protectiveness, warmth, and respect for another person. It is a deep feeling of affection and a lasting attraction that goes beyond the surface. Love is what turns into an emotional attachment.

On the other hand, lust is a physical attraction. Lust leads to an overwhelming feeling of sexual desire – thanks to a rush of hormones. You are focused more on the physical level rather than intellectual level. Lust will keep you living in a fantasy world, instead of dealing with the reality of your relationship. It will cause you to ignore all of the warning signs and take you down a road full of heartbreak.

Lust promotes unclean actions and dirty thoughts. It makes you lose focus and allows frustration to enter into your life. It will mislead you and affect your decision-making skills about everything – your relationships and your life. Lust will literally cause you to desire someone or something way too much. You will take

something good, twist it, and you will crave it until you are satisfied.

Hey girl, ask yourself this: How many times have I mistaken love for lust? If you can't properly distinguish the difference between love and lust, then you are in for world of hurt and confusion. You should always remember that lust wants to "get", while love longs to "give." There were many times when I thought I was in love, but in actuality, I was only in lust. I was just infatuated by the thought of being in love and loved by somebody. I gave so much of my time, money, attention, focus, and ultimately, myself to people. In the end, I did not get anything in return. After each encounter, I still felt like something was missing. Love is supposed to gratify you and leave you feeling fulfilled, not just physically, but mentally and spiritually.

Over time, I became so fed up with being broken, used, and abused. I knew I was a good person and wanted to welcome love into my heart, but was I really ready? I had to seriously ask myself that question and answer it. Honestly, the answer was a big NO! I didn't even love myself, so how could I determine and measure someone else's love for me? I understood that love was an action word, but what if words and actions didn't line up? What if the actions were conditional, or based on the words? My biggest problem was that I didn't value

or love myself enough. Because of that, it led me to feelings of unworthiness . I didn't feel like I deserved any of the love God had intended for me to have. I realized that because I was ignorant about what love really meant, I just accepted anything and anybody.

Hey girl, let me tell you, that led me down a road full of all types of abuse. I became a prisoner of pain. I walked around numb to my feelings, emotions, and life. I wasn't living, just existing. I realized that I had to do some self-examination and soul searching. I had to get to the root of my problems and issues. It was vital for me to "woman up" and make a conscious decision to change.

Chapter 2 Affirmations

Love vs. Lust

- I am loved by God with an everlasting love. Nothing shall separate me from the love of God.

- I am enough.

- I am worthy and deserving of love.

- I am rooted and grounded in love.

- I increase and abound in love.

- I love and accept myself.

- I am beautiful, smart, and strong.

Chapter 3

Embracing Change

What does it mean to embrace change? Well, before you can embrace change, you must identify and understand what change really is. Change is noted to make something different, to alter something, to modify and replace one thing with another. In other words, change means a different way of doing things. In order to embrace change, you have to be willing to operate and function differently than what you have in the past. Change

can't happen unless you are open and willing.

Now, let me honest, change isn't easy. It's scary but, girl, you must believe that you can do it. Change is something we tend to fear or become anxious about because we don't feel in control of our lives. Do not be afraid to try things a different way. If what you are doing hasn't been working for you, then what do you have to lose? Some things will never happen for you until you get yourself together and make a deliberate decision to change. When you embrace change, you can cultivate a positive attitude. By accepting change, you can start integrating it into your life without fear or regret. You are already aware of what doesn't work and what you don't like. So, you should be open to start new experiences with people, places, and things.

Instead of fearing change, you must embrace it. Change can be intimidating, but it is necessary for you to keep evolving, growing, and most importantly, going. You may feel overwhelmed, or even discouraged, on your journey towards change, but don't you dare quit. You have to allow change to empower, ignite, inspire, invoke, and propel you. There will be times when you will have to push yourself because the "old way" may seem or even feel better. Hey girl, remember if you want

better, you have to do better. If you want different, you have to do differently. If you want more, you have to do more. Embracing change requires discipline, consistency, and determination. What are you willing to change in order to produce better results in your life? When you learn to accept and embrace change, it will benefit and reward you in more ways than you could ever imagine.

When you finally decided to embrace change, your self-worth will increase and you won't accept anything less than what you deserve. While you're in the process of embracing change, you have to be rooted and grounded in your decision-making. You must change your thinking, way of doing things, and sometimes, your environment. Remember: embracing change is something that is totally new to you. Therefore, you will have to take it one day at a time.

While you are embracing and going through change, you will start to overcome obstacles and different adversities. The things that were once hard for you will become easier. Your sense of confidence will begin to intensify. You will start to understand that there's more to you than what meets the eye. The more your confidence rises, the more strength builds in your mind. When strength is built in your mind, fear and doubt have to be

pushed out. When you began to make the necessary changes to things you thought you couldn't, you will recognize just how strong of a woman you really are. You'll start to believe and trust in yourself more. Your self-esteem will exude from your very being.

Chapter 3 Affirmations

Embracing Change

- I do not fear change but embrace it.

- Things are changing in my life for the better.

- My worse days are over, and my best days are ahead of me.

- I give myself permission to change, grow, and evolve.

- I embrace the plan God has for my life, which is to prosper me and not to harm me.

- I embrace and trust the will of God for my life.

- I will not resist change because change is good, and it is necessary.

Chapter 4

Get A Grip

In this journey of life, you will experience unexpected and unforeseen circumstances that you never could've imagined. However, you must not lose focus or sight of who you are and who you are becoming. It's important to ask yourself these questions: How do I see myself? How do you identify yourself? Hey girl, that vision you have for yourself...don't lose it.

In order to maintain focus, you have to have a tight grip of who you are. In other

words, you must have a form of control over yourself and your life. You can't allow things, people, or situations in your life to control your very being. If you are, then girl, GET A GRIP! Don't give those things or people power over you. Listen, take your power back and get control of your life.

Often, power is given over to people and things because of unforgiveness. As a woman, it can sometimes be challenging for you to forgive. Being unable to forgive is not only challenging, but it's painful. It's a poison that pollutes your very being. If you want to keep a good grip of who you are, you have to forgive and stop holding onto things and people that do not contribute to the effectiveness of your life. Forgiveness is not for them, but it's for you and your sanity. When you forgive, you must not only forgive that person, but you also have to forgive the act that was done. In other words, forgive what was done and who it was done by. You can't forgive one and not the other. In order to completely be free, you have to forgive both sides. If not, you will continue to relive the acts that were done to you. If you refuse to forgive, then pain will be an unwanted guest in your life that. Yes, you may have been hurt, abandoned, rejected, lied on, and scandalized, but so what? Hey girl, get a grip! You are not what they did or said.

Your purpose in life is so much bigger than that and them.

I know what they said about you, but what do you say about you? Don't allow people's opinions of you place you in a box that you aren't currently in or created to live in. You have to stop walking around with a label that God didn't place on you. You're living your life by the opinions and validations of others. It's causing you to be frustrated, mad, upset, bitter, remorseful, and downright petty. Let it go! Let them go! Get a grip of yourself and take back control of your life.

On the other hand, it may not even be other people; it's your own self. You can be your own worst enemy. You have to forgive yourself. When you don't forgive yourself, you stay stuck in your past traumas and mistakes. You have to realize that you are not your mistakes. Yes, you've made mistakes, but it's time to "Woman Up!" Put your big girl panties on and make the necessary adjustments. You can't allow your past to hold you hostage, but you must live in your now and prepare for your future.

When you don't fully forgive yourself, resentment will start to take place. It will take root in your heart and mind, allowing bitterness to grow. At that moment, discouragement will try to creep in and rob you of your joy, contentment, and peace.

You'll start to build up ill feelings and damage your ability to give love to others, as well as receive love in return.

Chapter 4 Affirmations

Get A Grip

- I release what does not benefit my God given purpose.

- I will not hold on to what hinders me from God's plans for me.

- I'm focused on becoming a better me and will not get distracted.

- I acknowledge the truth about me and any situation concerning me.

- No longer will I allow my emotions to grip and control me.

- I release what had me and take control of what tried to control me.

- I will not give up when things get hard, but I will continue to move forward.

Chapter 5

Comparison Kills

Hey girl, let's be honest: change can sometimes be difficult and frustrating. You should be well aware that consistency is key. While you are on the journey to becoming who you're meant to be, you should never compare yourself or your process to anyone else. Why? Because comparison kills! Your journey has been tailor-made just for you. When you start comparing yourself, you diminish the value

of your story. Everyone has a story, but what makes yours so significant?

God created us equally but with unique differences. Even from a scientific standpoint, there is absolutely no one else in the world that has the same fingerprint as you. With that being said, you are something special and can never be duplicated or replaced. Hey girl, there will never be another you. You possess something that no other woman in the world has. So, don't you dare compare yourself to another woman.

Comparison can kill you in so many ways. It'll have you thinking that you are failing when you are really supposed to be learning and growing. Comparison can also cause you to adopt a false sense of who you are and who you should become. It will cause you to mirror your life after someone else's journey. Comparison is the thief of joy. When you start comparing yourself to others, you create a recipe for unhappiness, discomfort, envy, jealousy, and envy. Comparison allows another person to drive, dictate, and determine your behavior. You start maneuvering your life and making decisions according to how they live and move.

Hey girl, you can be anything, but you can't be everything! In order to truly be happy, you must operate and live according to how God designed for you to live. There

is one thing for sure that you are better at and that is being you. No one can do what you do or how you do it. You've got what it takes to "Woman Up." Hey girl, be authentically you because everyone else is already taken.

For me, comparison was an issue that I dealt with for many years. I was always the girl trying to fit in. In grade school, I was a little more on the heavier side due to medication I had to take. So, boys didn't really show any interest in me, like they did my friends. That really made me feel some type of way. So, I decided to act and dress differently, in hopes of seeking the attention of boys. I wanted all eyes on me. As a result, I opened a door to promiscuity and alcoholic.

My mother didn't raise me like that, so it wasn't a learned behavior. It was an adopted behavior. I allowed comparisons to consume and dictate the way I behaved. I knew better! And I knew that it wasn't me. However, I found something in being perceived as "wanted" and "needed. This false sense of desirability was my downfall. It seemed as though my friends were at their bests, and I was at my lowest, trying to keep up with them. Even though I appeared to be happy, I was struggling deep down inside.

My comparison phase spilled over from my teenage years into my early 20's. I always felt like I wasn't good enough. I constantly compared how I looked and lived against the other women around me. I would regularly change my hair, clothes, and demeanor to fit in. I spent countless days trying to be something that I wasn't. It never felt right. It just wasn't me. I found myself becoming bitter, angry, frustrated, and discouraged. I felt like such a failure and became fed up with my life. That was when I started drinking almost every day and clubbing every weekend. When I was under the influence, I wasn't in my right mind to even care about other people, their opinions, or their lives. I was the girl who got carried out of the club by Security. I was so incoherent and too drunk to do anything on my own accord.

The next day, when I had sobered up, I instantly felt disgusted and disappointed in myself. Not to mention, I would have the worst hangovers ever. I knew there had to be a different way of living. Why couldn't I be happy like everyone else? Was this really going to be my life? The more I tried to suppress my issues and insecurities, the bigger they became. I thought the issue was everybody else, but in actuality, it was ME. Every day I woke up with the same issue...ME. I struggled with who I thought I was, who I was trying to be, and who I was

actually meant to be. I was so busy looking at everybody else that I was confused about who I was. I was my own hinderance. I was the stumbling block that prevented me from being the fearfully and wonderfully woman God designed for me to be. At that moment, I knew it was time for me to "Woman Up!"

Chapter 5 Affirmations

Comparison Kills

- I am confident in myself and have no desire to be like others.

- I will not become envious or jealous of others.

- I am confident in who God has made me.

- I know, accept, and honor who I am.

- There is something unique about me that the world is waiting for.

- I will not compare my process with others because I have my own journey.

- My uniqueness is one of my greatest assets.

Chapter 6

Get Your Head Out of the Clouds

Now that you've realized that it's time for you to "Woman Up," you have to focus on your reality. Hey girl, get your head out of the clouds. In other words, stop daydreaming about who you want to become and fantasizing about the life you want to live. You must become aware and pay attention to what's happening around you. Not only should you focus on that, but you should also concentrate on what's happening *in* you. If you're honest with

yourself, you can admit that there are times when you are physically present, but your mind is somewhere else. You can be easily distracted from what's going on in your present state. As a result, you could become numb to your own feelings, emotions, happenings, and surroundings. You're in denial.

Denial can be a coping mechanism that keeps you in a dysfunctional cycle. It causes you to reject, resist, and refuse change. Hey girl, I told you earlier: you must embrace change. When you are in denial, you might try to protect yourself by not accepting the truth about you and what you are dealing with. However, instead of protecting yourself, you are really harming yourself and your future.

I know you might've had experiences that have been uncomfortable or possibly even traumatic. You have done everything in your power to try and forget those memories, to push your feelings aside. I'm sure there were even instances when you just wanted to pretend that nothing ever happened. Hey girl, snap out of it because it did happen! It might not have been your fault, but that doesn't negate the fact that it happened.

When you are in denial, you tend to feel comfortable in your dysfunctional life. You don't believe it can get any better. You

avoid confronting your feelings and circumstances instead of dealing with them. Denial may feel like the easier way out, but it will only magnify what you are dealing with. Denial makes it harder for change, grow, and evolve into the woman you need to be. At some point, you have to get to the root of the issue and face the reality of it. The more you avoid and distance yourself from your issues, the more you plunge deeper into denial. When you get deep into denial, it's hard to find your way out. You'll find yourself becoming isolated, broken, shattered, and just stuck. It's almost like being trapped in a box and you can't figure out how to get out of it.

During a certain period in my life, I was in denial about my relationships, decisions, and even myself. The crazy part is that I had no idea I was denial. Since I wasn't cognizant of it, I felt stuck in a vicious cycle and ignorant of my value as a woman. I allowed things to be said and done to me that I shouldn't have. I tolerated too much for too long. I had to realize that I had the power, the authority, and the right to determine how someone treated me by what I accepted. If they didn't agree or like it, then that meant they didn't want to be in my life. Once I understood that concept, my cutoff game got stronger and stronger. My friends began to change, my

environment began to change, and my mindset began to change. Once those things started changing, my life began to change for the better as well. After I snapped out of denial, I could face the reality of my issues.

Now, denial is not always easy to overcome. When I was younger, there was this guy I wanted. For many years, I did everything to prove that I was the one for him. I went out of my way to do things for him and did everything I could to please him. Whenever he called, I would drop whatever I was doing and go running. The level of denial was through the roof. He did just enough to string me along and kept me hanging there. He said what I wanted to hear and gave me false hope that he had every intention for us to be together. He was manipulating me and had no remorse for it. On top of everything, while we were together, this man had children with several different women. Hey girl, was I stupid or what?

I had to come to the conclusion that he and I were on two separate pages were never going to be together. It became evident that he didn't want me, just what I could do for him. So yes, I was stupid, but also, in deep denial.

It is possible to pull yourself out of denial, but you have to be intentional about it. In order to conquer denial, you have to

learn to love yourself without restraints. When you're in denial, it takes something extremely life changing to make you realize the severity of your situation. Those life changing events will help you to see the real truth. Guess what? The truth will hurt, but it will also emancipate you from the dangers of denial. Once you are free, you can began working on you, girl.

Chapter 6 Affirmations

Get Your Head Out of the Clouds

- I will not be deceived by vain words spoken to me.

- I am not blind to my reality and will not live in a fantasy world.

- My eyes are open to all schemes, plots, and traps that try to hinder me in life.

- I am alert and aware of the way I live my life.

- I will not lie to myself or others.

- I am strong enough to make all the decisions I need to make.

- I will not allow anyone or anything to manipulate me.

Chapter 7

Pick Up Your Feelings

Once you conquer the denial phase, you are ready to pick up your feelings and reestablish the woman you are. It's never too late to start over. Sometimes, things have to be torn down in order to be put back together the correct way. When you go through things, it leaves you feeling some type of way. There will be situations when you will have to ask yourself, "Who, or what, has me upset?" Then, you need to ask yourself if it or they can alter the

purpose of your life. If you answered, "Yes," then whatever it is has too much power over you and your emotions. You are too emotionally driven and it's time to take your power back. Hey girl, pick up your feelings and let's move forward.

I want to empower you to be great and function in the best version of yourself, but you can't do that as long as you are stuck in your feelings. You don't have the time or space to be caught in your feelings. You may cry but don't quit. One of the worst mistakes you can make is to quit on yourself. Failure is not an option, but it is a choice.

There may be times when things seem hard. You might start to question whether you have what it takes to become a better version of you or not. During those times, you can't allow self-doubt to sneak into your mind. Self-doubt is the quickest way to fail yourself. It will trigger you to abort the mission of changing. You'll start doubting yourself and your ability to change when you are presented with obstacles. Remember: tough times never last but tough people do.

It might feel as though the world has turned against you. All you can see are your problems, circumstances, and challenges. Hey girl, don't you dare quit. Keep moving forward! Obstacles are presented to test your perseverance. You

must never faint, lose hope, or succumb to your emotions at that moment. You can't allow yourself to be emotionally driven. Your emotions can and will lie to you. Since emotions can lie, you must understand how to bring your emotions under subjection. You have to believe in yourself at all times. When you feel like giving up, remember the times when you were faced with adversity and you overcame them. If you've done it before, you most certainly can do it again.

On this journey to "Woman Up," you will be met with challenges. No matter what challenges you encounter along the way, your mindset must be: *I can do this.* If you change your mindset, you'll change your thoughts. If you change your thoughts, you'll change your words. If you change your words, then you'll change your life. Your words ultimately change your world. Your mindset determines if you will give up or keep pressing forward. It is necessary for you to have self-motivation.

Self-motivation is the force that keeps pushing and propelling you forward. It's also an internal drive that pushes you to achieve, produce, develop, and continue to move onward. You may find it difficult to stay motivated because making a change in your life requires persistence, discipline, and dedication. Changing your life is hard work, but necessary when evolving into a

greater woman. It's common to feel frustrated, especially when change isn't happening as quickly as you would like it to. However, you must not give in to defeat but stay focused.

Self-motivation will keep you focused since it is the "why" behind everything that you are doing. It's the reason you've committed to changing. It requires you to believe in yourself even when no one else does. Others may count you out, but you can't count yourself out. Self-motivation keeps you going, despite any setbacks that may present themselves to you and it assists you with following through on making the necessary changes you need to make. In other words, it's all about having the grit. Grit will take you farther than you think. As a matter of fact, grit will take you all the way to the finish line.

During this process, it's important to examine what is motivating you to go after change. Why do you want change? What's your reason for changing? The clearer you are on your "why," the easier it will be to stay focused on the work you're doing and to create the life you want. Finding self-motivation requires long-standing commitment, courage, and perseverance.

Hey girl, you already have it in you. Now, all you have to do is pick up your feelings, get them in check, and start moving forward. Once again, failure is not

an option, but it is a choice. What will your choice be?

Chapter 7 Affirmations

Pick Up Your Feelings

- I allow myself to release all negative emotions which no longer serve me.

- I free myself of all emotions that are not mine to carry.

- I release all hurt, rejection, fear, anger, wrath, sadness, depression, discouragement, grief, bitterness, and

unforgiveness that I have been holding on to.

- o I will not be led by my emotions.
- o My emotions do not control me, but I control them.
- o My emotions will not get the best of me.
- o I am emotionally stable.

Chapter 8

It's Time for Take-Off

Hey girl, guess what? You have been given the tools to "Woman Up" and live a better life. It's time for you to use them and soar. You are now ready for take-off. Your pain prepared you for your God-given purpose. The things you've experienced were just seasonal. Seasons are meant to change, and change is here. You have now entered into a new season. Hey girl, embrace it! Always remember that seasons change, styles change, people change, and

systems changes. However, God never changes. He is always here to help you along your journey. You must have faith in God and trust His plan for your life. It takes more energy to live a life full of fear than to live one full of faith. When you're afraid, you've convinced yourself to live inside the walls you've built for yourself. When you have faith, you can assure yourself to embrace change.

You can either live in faith or live-in fear. However, faith and fear cannot coexist and occupy the same space. When your desire to overcome becomes greater than your fear, you'll conquer adversity effortlessly. Fear will always attempt to immobilize you, while faith is designed to energize you.

God wants to do a new thing in your life right now. That's right, girl, right now. He designed you to be a woman full of love, life, and joy. He wants you to live in abundance above the drama, chaos, and confusion. You were not created to be broken, depressed, or confused. It's not impossible to live out God's intention for you. You just have "Woman Up" and put in the work. If you make one step, then He'll make two. Stop making excuses for why you can't do it. No more excuses. Excuses are the lies you tell yourself when you're too afraid of the future and change. Excuses

will always keep you in a limited place. Overcoming adversity is impossible when you're making excuses. You can conquer excuses by having the courage to step out.

God will help you put the pieces of your heart, emotions, and mind back together. Broken crayons still color. Have you ever heard of that saying? It simply means that in spite of everything you have been through, you still have value and a purpose. You were born on purpose for a purpose. God gave you the stamina to stand through any storm that life brings your way, as well as the tenacity to triumph, even in moments of great turbulence.

Listen, girl, fasten your seatbelt and get ready to take off! What you went through was not in vain but orchestrated to help make you into the phenomenal woman that you are or will be. It qualified you to live your best life and function at your highest potential. You fought hard to get to this point, but don't stop here because there is more for you. What was holding you is now exposed, confronted, and demolished. You are UNSTOPPABLE! Your worst days are behind you and your best days are ahead of you. Hey girl, better is the end of a thing than the beginning.

It's not about how you started but how you finish. It's time to finish this

journey stronger than ever. You won't look like what you have been through. All of the pain, shame, and embarrassment was necessary for you to develop into an amazing woman. Congratulations for making it through some of the toughest times of your life. You go girl! You are a force to be reckoned with. You are unshakeable. There were some moments when life just knocked the wind out of you, but now, you can breathe again. What didn't kill you, only made you stronger.

Life will try to get you down and out, but you can gather yourself back up. You must learn and not be limited by the experiences of your life. You are strong and have a dreamer inside of you. Anything is possible if you are willing to persevere. Overcoming adversity is the secret of champions. When you have the right mindset, don't make excuses or take no for an answer, you can overcome anything that life has to throw at you. Have faith and be empowered by success.

Don't forget the sacrifices that have been made. You've come too far to turn around now. Stop looking in the rearview mirror at your past. Keep the car in drive and press the gas to go full speed ahead. You have a destination called "Purpose," and you have to get there. Now that you are prepared for take-off, you can't be

distracted by delays, layovers, or other people's tickets. You have all the tools you need to spread your wings and soar.

Hey girl, all that's left to do is "Woman UP."

Chapter 8 Affirmations

It's Time for Take off

- I can do anything I put my mind to and be successful.

- I'm ready to become the woman God has purposed for me to be.

- I'm ready to Woman Up and take my life back.

- No longer will I allow my past to hold me captive.

- I am unstoppable.

- This is my season and my time.

- I do not fear the fire because I am the fire.

Acknowledgements

To my children – Isaiah, Joel, Destini, and Gracelyn – I thank God for allowing me to birth. You all add so much joy and purpose to my life. I love you guys so much.

To my mother – Where would I be without you? You are the epitome of what it means to "Woman Up". Lord knows I appreciate your prayers and encouragement. I strive every day to be an

exceptional woman just like you. I love you mom.

To my spiritual parents – Apostle Travis Jennings and Dr. Stephanie Jennings—There aren't enough words to express my appreciation. Thank you for speaking life and purpose into me. I'm so grateful for what you have poured and continually to pour into me.

Connect with the Author

Facebook:Dria Cobb

Instagram: the_dria_cobb

www.ingramcontent.com/pod-product-compliance
Lightning Source LLC
Chambersburg PA
CBHW071839290426
44109CB00017B/1864